D0535665

OLIVES

A Book of Recipes

INTRODUCTION BY PEPITA ARIS

LORENZ BOOKS

LONDON • NEW YORK • SYDNEY • BATH

First published by Lorenz Books in 1996

© 1996 Anness Publishing Limited

Lorenz Books is an imprint of
Anness Publishing Limited
Boundary Row Studios
1 Boundary Row
London SE1 8HP

This edition distributed in Canada by
Raincoast Books Distribution Limited

Distributed in Australia by Reed Books Australia

ISBN 1 85967 162 4

Publisher Joanna Lorenz
Senior Cookery Editor Linda Fraser
Cookery Editor Anne Hildyard
Designer Lilian Lindblom
Illustrations Anna Koska
Photographers Karl Adamson, Edward Allwright, Steve Baxter, James Duncan,
Michelle Garrett and Amanda Heywood
Recipes Alex Barker, Maxine Clark, Carole Clements, Elizabeth Wolf-Cohen, Sarah Gates, Shirley Gill,
Carole Handslip, Annie Nichols, Liz Trigg and Steven Wheeler

Typeset by MC Typeset Ltd, Rochester, Kent
Printed in Singapore by Star Standard Industries Pte. Ltd.

Jacket photography Amanda Heywood

For all recipes, quantities are given in both metric and imperial measures and, where appropriate,
measures are also given in standard cups and spoons. Follow one set, but not a mixture,
because they are not interchangeable.

OLIVES

Contents

$\mathcal{I}$NTRODUCTION

Black olives were described by Lawrence Durrell as: "A taste older than meat, older than wine. A taste as old as cold water". The silver-grey olive tree has probably been cultivated around the Mediterranean for 8,000 years and the trees live long: the olives of the Garden of Gethsamane are still there; in the heart of Majorca some trees may be 1,000 years old. The olive tree was once the mainstay of Mediterranean life; the olive flourishes where nothing else will grow, and bread and olives were once the diet of the poor. Today, olives and olive oil, with pasta, vegetables and fruit, are the keynote of the Mediterranean Diet, which holds out a hope of improved health for us all.

A choice of green or black olives is standard with apéritifs, but the real variety is amazing. Tiniest are the Spanish *Arbequines*, a medley of green or purplish-grey, with a hint of rosemary. The medium-size, oil-rich *Manzanilla* is Spain's and California's main olive. Look out for huge green Spanish *Gordals del rey* ("the king's fat ones"), often perversely labelled "Queen's", and brine-packed *Perlas* from Aragon, French irregular, green *Picholines*, large, black, brined *Tanche* and smaller reddish-brown *Nyons* olives, Italian dull bronze-green *Calabreses* and the Sicilian-style small cracked olives in brine, stuffed with red pepper.

Best of all, many think, are the extra large purple *Kalamata* olives from Greece, with the flavour of the red wine vinegar used to cure them. Black Greek olives in brine are the model for Californian *Alfonso* olives.

Of the 700 or so varieties, some are favoured for oil and others for table olives. The range of olive colours largely reflects the stage of picking: green olives are unripe, firm and less oily; purply brown ones are ripe and the black ones are overripe, with a much softer texture, and mainly used for oil. A wrinkled olive will probably be sun-dried.

The first person who, having tasted a wild olive, saw it as a crop, must have been a man of vision, for the olive on a tree is decidedly bitter. They are treated to remove bitterness before curing.

Olives have an affinity with many ingredients, as is demonstrated by the variety of recipes in this book. As well as featuring heavily in starters and salads, they provide a pungent counterpoint to delicate fish and shellfish, they also set off richer meats, such as duck and beef. Their intense flavour provides a welcome punctuation in blander dishes using pasta, grains and breads. Olives have a highly versatile role in the kitchen, and this collection of the best of olive recipes, will inspire you to make the most of them.

TYPES OF OLIVE

There are literally hundreds of varieties of olives and, just as grapes are grown depending on whether they are intended for the table or for wine, so olives are grown either for eating or for pressing into oil. Different varieties are also grown according to climate, soil and other geographical conditions, so that the olives you find in most supermarkets are usually only classified by their country of origin. Greek and Italian olives are reckoned to be the finest, although France and Spain also grow some deservedly renowned olives and these are well worth looking out for.

GREEN OLIVES

Whether olives are green or black is not a matter of type but of timing – all olives are green at first, they are simply the unripe fruit of the tree. Green olives contain less oil, which explains why they have a sharper flavour and firmer flesh than the fully ripened black olive. Being unripe, green olives are inedible

unless they are treated to remove their bitter and indigestible starches. Commercially, this is done by immersing olives in a soda solution and then packing them in brine. However local growers often prepare their own olives, washing them every day for about 10 days in fresh water and then storing them in earthenware jars of brine mixed with herbs, spices and other aromatic ingredients. They are then left for up to a year to develop their distinctive colour and smooth texture. Consequently, locally purchased green olives are often quite different from the commercially bought variety and a great deal of fun can be had, too, trying to coax the exact recipe from a secretive Greek or Italian olive grower!

BLACK OLIVES

These fully ripe olives, being full of oil, are more rounded in flavour and softer-fleshed than green olives. They are picked when fully ripe, then fermented and oxidised to give a glossy black finish.

BROWN OR PURPLE OLIVES

These are simply olives caught halfway between green and black. They have more of the characteristic mellow flavour of the black olive, yet still retain a subtle sharpness.

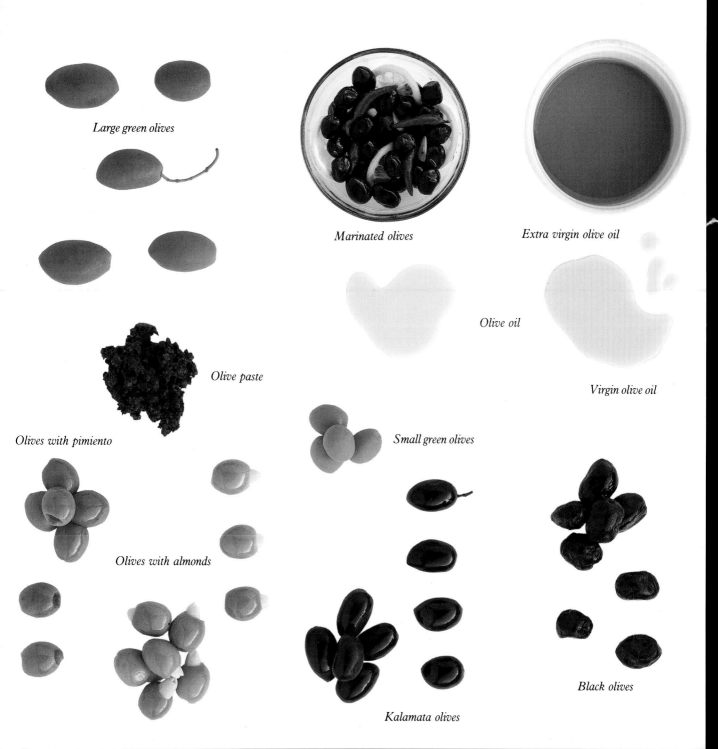

Large green olives

Marinated olives

Extra virgin olive oil

Olive oil

Virgin olive oil

Olive paste

Olives with pimiento

Small green olives

Olives with almonds

Black olives

Kalamata olives

$\mathcal{O}$LIVE $\mathcal{V}$ARIETIES

ITALY

Italy is one of the biggest olive-producing countries in the world and consequently has the greatest diversity of olives. Almost every region grows olives, and while for most growers the challenge is to produce the best olive oil, many farmers pride themselves on cultivating trees for the olives alone. The large green *Cerignola* or the black olives from *Castellamare* are likely to go on top of pizzas; they are the tiny black wrinkled olives from around Rome. Since different regions give their olives different names, it is difficult to single out any particular variety.

SPAIN

Most olives come from Andalusia. The best known green table olive is the *Manzanilla*. This is most likely to be the olive you buy under the label Spanish olive and is also likely to be the variety stuffed with pimiento or almonds. The *Gordal* or *Queen* is the largest and most fleshy green or black Spanish olive.

FRANCE

Provence is the area best known for olive growing in France, an area loved by painters and gourmets alike for its rolling landscape of vines and olive groves. Olives are part of the French way of life and appear in a wide variety of recipes, as well as simply served as appetizers. *Picholine* is the main green olive. It is small and long, with a tasty flavour and firm flesh. *Lucques*, another excellent table olive, is long and slightly curved with green and slightly glossy flesh. Introduced to Provence, the Ardeche and Corsica after an extremely damaging winter in 1956, *Tanche* is a large and delicious black olive, used for its oil but also served in its own right as an appetiser.

GREECE

Green and black olives are served in abundance in Greece, as appetizers or mezes and it is unusual to be served an ouzo or Retsina without a little bowl of glossy, aromatic olives. Olives are grown throughout the country and are perfectly adapted to the hot dry summers.

MEDITERRANEAN FAVOURITES

LINGUINE WITH OLIVES AND CAPERS

This famous dish from Naples is known as Linguine alla Puttanesca *in Italian, the name* puttana *coming from the Italian word for prostitute. Why, no one knows, but it is very good nonetheless.*

Fry a finely chopped clove of garlic in 30ml/2 tbsp olive oil, then add 2–3 chopped anchovy fillets, 15ml/2 tbsp capers, 16 stoned black olives, 4 chopped tomatoes and a little seasoning. Cook for about 5 minutes, stirring frequently. Boil 400g/14oz linguine, drain and add the olive sauce. Serves 4.

GREEN OLIVE PASTE

This Spanish version of tapenade uses green olives instead of black ones and is delicious spread thinly on slices of bread.

Place 40 green olives, 5ml/1 tsp capers, 4 anchovies, 5ml/1 tsp ground almonds, 1 garlic clove, 60ml/4 tbsp olive oil and a pinch of ground cumin and paprika in a food processor. Blend to a fine paste.

PISSALADIERE

This quick French version of an Italian pizza is native to Nice.

Roll out 225g/8oz shortcrust pastry and line a 30cm/12in baking tray. Fry 1.2kg/2½lb finely sliced onions and 2 crushed garlic cloves in a little olive oil until the onions are soft but not brown. Top the pastry with the onions and decorate with 14 stoned black olives and 10 anchovy fillets. Dribble a little extra olive oil over the top and bake at 200°C/400°F/Gas 6 for 20–22 minutes until the pastry is cooked. Serves 4.

GREEK COUNTRY SALAD

A great Greek favourite, served preferably with Retsina.

Arrange 3 tomatoes, cut into wedges, ½ peeled and sliced cucumber and 1 thinly sliced mild onion in a salad bowl. Pour over 60ml/4 tbsp olive oil, salt and plenty of freshly ground black pepper and then sprinkle with 150g/5oz crumbled feta cheese and 14 stoned black olives and a good pinch of oregano. Toss lightly together. Serves 4.

PRESERVING OLIVES

If you buy too many olives and do not use them all at once, or if you simply want to refresh some canned or bottled olives, here are a few simple but delicious recipes which can't fail to liven up a jaded palate.

GARLIC OLIVES

Drain a jar of green olives in brine, keeping half the brine. Pack the jar with the olives, 2 crushed garlic cloves and a pinch of oregano. Mix the brine with enough olive oil and white wine vinegar to fill the jar and pour over the olives. Leave for a couple of weeks in the fridge.

CRACKED GREEN OLIVES

Cut a cross at the top and bottom of 450g/1lb green olives, cutting right through to the stone. Place a layer of olives in the bottom of one large, or several smaller jars, and sprinkle with 15ml/1 tbsp coriander seeds. Add a garlic clove and 10ml/2 tsp oregano and continue making layers, leaving a good 2.5cm/1in at the top of the jar. Fill with olive oil, cover tightly and leave to marinate for at least 2–3 weeks.

TAPENADE   Serves 4

This famous black olive paste from Provence takes its name from the French word for capers.

Place 350g/12oz stoned black olives, 1 can anchovies plus their oil, 30ml/2 tbsp capers, 1–2 crushed garlic cloves, 5ml/1 tsp chopped fresh thyme, 15ml/1 tbsp Dijon mustard, juice ½ lemon and 45ml/3 tbsp olive oil in a food processor and blend until smooth. Turn into a dish and chill slightly before serving. Tapenade will keep for several days in a pot sealed with a layer of olive oil. Serve the tapenade spread on bread or crackers, as a dip for crisp vegetable sticks, or stir into hot pasta for a quick sauce.

M A R I N A T E D   B L A C K   O L I V E S

Mix 450g/1lb black olives with 30ml/2 tbsp red wine vinegar, 1 garlic clove, 1 or 2 whole red chillies or a pinch of chilli powder and 3–4 slices of lemon. Turn into a large jar or several smaller jars and add sufficient olive oil to cover the olives. Cover tightly and leave for 2–3 weeks at room temperature. Eat on their own, or add to casseroles or salads.

Stuffed Olive Varieties

● Green olives with pimiento – the deep red pepper contrasts beautifully with the green of the olive, while the flavour is mild but distinctive.

● Green olives with almonds – a favourite Spanish stuffing, the almond adds an intriguing and pleasant crunchy texture.

● Green olives with onion – another Spanish favourite.

● Green olives with garlic – a good cocktail olive, with a distinct flavour.

● Green olives with anchovies – a quite delicious, salty olive, popular in the south of France.

● Green olives with capers – unusual and worth looking out for in delicatessens.

● Green olives with orange or lemon peel – the citrus peel adds a distinct and contrasting flavour to the olives.

● Green olives with black olives – a fairly uncommon combination, it's interesting to try and distinguish between the two.

PREPARING OLIVES

To stone olives, use an olive or cherry stoner, sometimes called a chasse noyer. *It looks a bit like a leather puncher and works in a similar way. Place the base of the olive on the base of the stoner, so that the plunger sits over the top. Press firmly and the stone will be ejected.*

Olives, particularly black ones, can be easily stoned by hand. Using a sharp knife, cut the flesh from top to bottom down to the stone. Push the flesh back and ease the stone out.

Stuffed olives make attractive garnishes, particularly pimiento-stuffed olives, since the red and green contrast nicely. Cut horizontally into thin slices and use to decorate fresh salmon, tuna dishes or salads. They also look pretty set into savoury mousses or topping meat or fish pâtés.

COOK'S TIPS

• For added flavour, add green olives to meat casseroles and stews.

• Add stoned, halved black olives to *gremolata* – a mixture of chopped parsley, lemon rind and crushed garlic. Mix with a little extra virgin olive oil and serve with hot pasta.

• When making garlic bread, spread some olive paste between the slices before baking.

• Add chopped black olives to a vinaigrette dressing and serve with a light green salad.

• Use strips of olive to garnish savoury dishes.

OLIVE OIL

The history of olive oil is literally centuries old, woven deeply into myths and legends, so that for the people of the Mediterranean, such as the Greeks and the Italians, olive oil is as much part of their culture as the Parthenon in Athens or the Colosseum in Rome.

Of all oils used in cooking, olive oil is considered to be the healthiest. It is principally a monounsaturated fat which experts believe actually helps reduce cholesterol levels in the body. It also contains a high proportion of vitamin A.

Olive oils have as many flavours as there are varieties of olives. For the uninitiated, it is an almost impossible task to know what is a good oil, and each oil-producing country has its own system of labelling and grading. Colours vary from green to golden, yet are no indication of the quality of the oil, since it depends on where the olives were harvested. Connoisseurs have strong feelings about olive oil, describing it in all sorts of flowery ways, from grass and apple (probably good) to cucumber (not so good) and rough or rancid (definitely bad). For those who are unsure about which olive oil to choose from the large selection available, the best method is to sample them in a hot dish or salad, then decide whether the flavour is one you prefer.

EXTRA VIRGIN OLIVE OIL

The very best and most expensive olive oil, from whatever country it comes from, is virgin oil from the first cold pressing. It is usually a greenish colour, but may also be golden yellow. Don't waste it in frying; use it in salads and mayonnaise where you can best appreciate its exquisite mellow, fruity flavour.

VIRGIN OIL

Extra virgin has no more than 1 per cent oleic acid, while "virgin oil" has up to 4 per cent. For professionals, the less acid the finer the oil.

PURE OLIVE OIL

This is a blend of cold-pressed virgin oil and refined olive oil that has been treated with chemicals and then heated and filtered. The colour of the oil is normally paler and the flavour blander and less distinctive. Light olive oil, which has a very mild flavour, is produced from the last pressing, and has the same nutritional values as pure olive oil. Because these oils are blended, each bottle will have the same mild flavour. While the professional olive oil connoisseur wouldn't give these oils house room, they are perfectly suitable for cooking purposes. Where more flavour is required, for salad dressings or pasta sauces, virgin or extra virgin olive oil is the best option for an authentic Mediterranean taste.

15

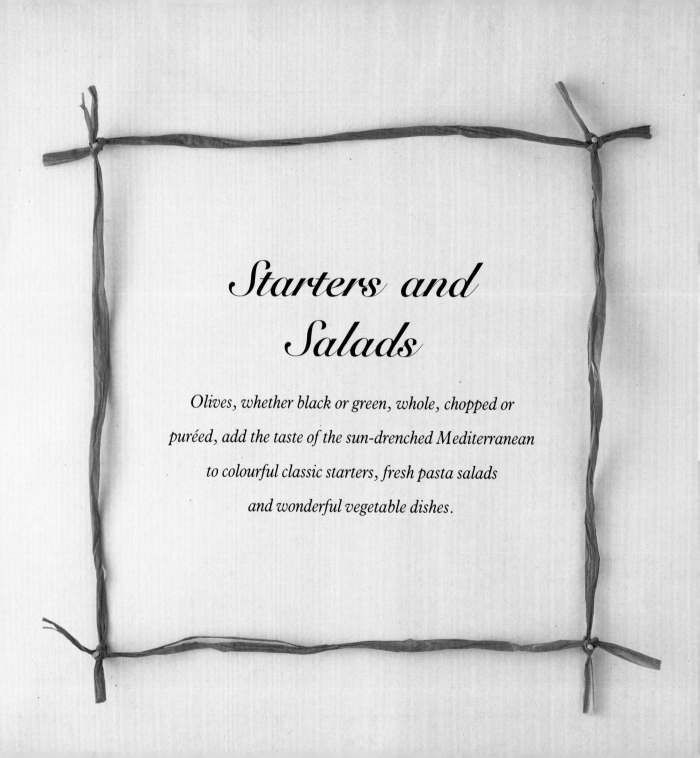

Starters and Salads

Olives, whether black or green, whole, chopped or
puréed, add the taste of the sun-drenched Mediterranean
to colourful classic starters, fresh pasta salads
and wonderful vegetable dishes.

GRILLED PEPPER AND OLIVE SALAD

This colourful, sunny salad was created in southern Italy, from locally grown ingredients.

Serves 6

*4 large peppers, red, yellow, green, or a
combination of all three*

*30ml/2 tbsp capers in salt, vinegar or
brine, rinsed*

18–20 black or green olives, stoned

For the dressing

90ml/6 tbsp extra virgin olive oil

2 garlic cloves, finely chopped

*30ml/2 tbsp balsamic or white
wine vinegar*

salt and ground black pepper

Place the peppers under a hot grill, and turn occasionally until they are black and blistered on all sides. Remove from the heat and leave for about 20 minutes to cool.

Peel the peppers, then cut into quarters. Remove the stems and seeds. Cut the peppers into strips, and arrange them in a serving dish. Distribute the capers and olives evenly over the peppers.

For the dressing, mix the oil and garlic together in a small bowl, crushing the garlic with a spoon to release as much flavour as possible. Mix in the vinegar, and season with salt and pepper. Pour over the peppers, mix well, and allow to stand for at least 30 minutes before serving.

COOK'S TIP

*After the peppers are grilled,
place in a polythene bag or cover
with a damp cloth, then leave
until cool. The steam loosens the
skin, making peeling easier.*

SALADE NICOISE

There are probably as many versions of this salad as there are cooks in Provence. With good French bread, this makes a wonderful summer lunch or light supper.

Serves 4–6
225g/8oz French beans
450g/1lb new potatoes
white wine vinegar and olive oil,
  for sprinkling
1 small Cos or round lettuce
4 ripe plum tomatoes, quartered
1 small cucumber, peeled and diced
1 green or red pepper, thinly sliced
4 hard-boiled eggs, quartered
24 Niçoise or black olives, stoned
225g/8oz can tuna in brine, drained
50g/2oz can anchovy fillets in olive oil
basil leaves, to garnish
garlic croûtons, to serve

For the anchovy vinaigrette
15ml/1 heaped tbsp Dijon mustard
50g/2oz can anchovy fillets in olive oil
1 garlic clove, crushed
60ml/4 tbsp lemon juice
120ml/4fl oz/1/2 cup sunflower oil
120ml/4fl oz/1/2 cup virgin olive oil
ground black pepper

First make the anchovy vinaigrette. Place the mustard, the anchovies with their oil, and garlic in a bowl. Blend together by pressing the garlic and anchovies against the sides of the bowl. Season generously with pepper. Using a small whisk, blend in the lemon juice. Slowly whisk in the sunflower oil in a thin stream and then the olive oil, whisking until the dressing is smooth and creamy.

Alternatively, put all the ingredients except the oil in a blender or food processor fitted with the metal blade and process to combine. With the machine running, add the oils in a thin stream until the vinaigrette is thick and creamy.

Drop the French beans into a large saucepan of boiling water and boil for 3 minutes until tender, yet crisp. Transfer the beans to a colander with a slotted spoon, then rinse under cold running water. Drain again and set aside. Cut the potatoes into 2.5cm/1in pieces and add them to the same boiling water, reduce the heat and simmer for 10–15 minutes until just tender, then drain. Sprinkle with a little vinegar and olive oil and a spoonful of the vinaigrette. Tear the lettuce into pieces and arrange on a platter, top with the tomatoes, cucumber and pepper, then add the French beans and potatoes. Place the eggs around the edge of the platter, arrange the olives, tuna and anchovies on top and garnish with the basil leaves. Drizzle with the remaining vinaigrette and serve with garlic croûtons.

TAPENADE AND QUAIL'S EGGS

Tapenade, a purée made from capers, olives and anchovies, is an excellent partner to eggs. You can use hen's eggs, but quail's eggs look very pretty on open sandwiches.

Makes 8

8 quail's eggs

1 small baguette

a few leaves curly endive

3 small tomatoes, sliced

4 canned anchovy fillets, halved
lengthways

black olives, stoned

parsley sprigs, to garnish

For the tapenade

90g/3¹/₂oz can tuna, drained

25g/1oz/1¹/₂ tbsp capers

10 canned anchovy fillets

75g/3oz/³/₄ cup black olives, stoned

60ml/4 tbsp olive oil

Boil the quail's eggs for 5 minutes, then plunge straight into cold water to cool. Crack the shells and remove them very carefully.

To make the tapenade, place the tuna, capers, anchovies and olives in a blender or food processor and blend until smooth, scraping down the sides when necessary. Gradually add the oil through the feeder tube and mix well. Cut the baguette into diagonal slices and spread each slice with a little of the tapenade. Arrange the curly endive and tomato slices on top. Halve the quail's eggs and place over the tomato.

Spoon a little more tapenade on to each quail egg, then add the anchovies and olives. Garnish with small parsley sprigs.

TOMATO, CHEESE AND OLIVE SALAD

Sweet sun-ripened tomatoes are delicious when served with feta cheese and olive oil. This salad, popular in Greece and Turkey, is enjoyed as a light meal with pieces of crispy bread.

Serves 4

900g/2lb tomatoes
200g/7oz feta cheese
120ml/4fl oz/½ cup olive oil,
*   preferably Greek*
12 black olives, stoned
ground black pepper

COOK'S TIP
Feta cheese has a strong flavour and is very salty. The freshest varieties are imported from Greece and are available from specialist delicatessens.

Carefully remove the tough cores from the tomatoes with a small sharp knife. Slice the tomatoes thickly and arrange in a shallow dish.

Crumble the cheese over the tomatoes, sprinkle with the olive oil, then sprinkle with the black olives. Season with freshly ground black pepper and serve the salad at room temperature.

21

CHEESE AND OLIVE-STUFFED PEARS

Pears, with a cheese and olive filling, make a sublime dish when served with a simple salad.

Serves 4

50g/2oz/¼ cup ricotta cheese

50g/2oz/¼ cup dolcelatte cheese

15ml/1 tbsp clear honey

½ celery stick, finely sliced

*12 green olives, stoned and roughly
  chopped*

4 dates, stoned and cut into thin strips

pinch of paprika

4 ripe pears

150ml/¼ pint/⅔ cup apple juice

Preheat the oven to 200°C/400°F/Gas 6. Place the ricotta in a bowl and crumble in the dolcelatte. Add the rest of the ingredients except for the pears and apple juice and mix well.

Halve the pears lengthways and use a melon baller to remove the cores. Place in an ovenproof dish and divide the filling equally between them.

Pour in the apple juice and cover the dish with foil. Bake for 20 minutes or until the pears are tender.

Remove the foil and place the dish under a hot grill for 3 minutes. Transfer to serving plates and serve immediately.

COOK'S TIP

*Choose ripe pears in season
such as Conference, William
or Comice.*

22

CAPONATA

A rich, spicy mixture of aubergines, tomatoes, capers and olives, Caponata is a part of Sicilian antipasti.

Serves 4

60ml/4 tbsp olive oil

1 large onion, sliced

2 celery sticks, sliced

450g/1lb aubergines, diced

5 ripe tomatoes, chopped

1 garlic clove, crushed

45ml/3 tbsp red wine vinegar

15ml/1 tbsp sugar

30ml/2 tbsp capers

12 olives, stoned

pinch of salt

60ml/4 tbsp chopped fresh parsley,
   to garnish

warm crusty bread and marinated
   olives, to serve

Heat half the oil in a large heavy saucepan. Add the onion and celery and cook over a gentle heat for about 3–4 minutes to soften.

Add the remainder of the oil with the aubergine and stir to absorb the oil. Cook until the aubergine begins to colour, then add the chopped tomatoes, garlic, vinegar and sugar.

Cover the surface of the vegetables with a circle of greaseproof paper and simmer for 8–10 minutes.

Add the capers and olives, then season to taste with salt. Turn the Caponata out into a bowl, garnish with parsley and serve at room temperature with warm crusty bread and olives.

COOK'S TIP

Anchovies and pine nuts also make good additions to Caponata. Add with the capers but omit the salt.

Pasta Salad with Sun-dried Tomatoes and Olives

This delicious salad combines the flavours of the Mediterranean and is an excellent way of serving pasta.

Serves 6

*450g/1lb pasta, such as shells, farfalle
or penne*
60ml/4 tbsp extra virgin olive oil
10 sun-dried tomatoes, thinly sliced
30ml/2 tbsp capers, in brine or salted
115g/4oz/1 cup black olives, stoned
2 garlic cloves, finely chopped
45ml/3 tbsp balsamic vinegar
45ml/3 tbsp chopped fresh parsley
salt and ground black pepper

Cook the pasta in a large pan of rapidly boiling salted water until it is *al dente*. Drain, and rinse under cold water to stop further cooking. Drain well and turn into a large bowl. Toss with the olive oil, and set aside.

Soak the tomatoes in a bowl of hot water for 10 minutes. Do not discard the water. Rinse the capers well. If they have been preserved in salt, soak them in a little hot water for 10 minutes. Rinse again.

Combine the olives, tomatoes, capers, garlic and vinegar in a small bowl. Season with salt and pepper.

Stir this mixture into the pasta, and toss well. Add 2 or 3 spoons of the tomato soaking water if the salad seems too dry. Toss with the parsley, and allow to stand for 15 minutes before serving.

COOK'S TIP

*If you prefer, use sun-dried
tomato paste instead of the
whole sun-dried tomatoes. Add
60ml/4 tbsp sun-dried tomato
paste, with 30ml/2 tbsp water.*

TOMATOES WITH OLIVE STUFFING

The versatile tomato is one of Italy's staple foods, appearing in more than three-quarters of all Italian savoury dishes. In this flavourful recipe, they are stuffed with olives, herbs and cheese, then baked.

Serves 4

8 large tomatoes, firm and ripe

115g/4oz/1¼ cups small soup pasta

8 black olives, stoned and finely
  chopped

45ml/3 tbsp finely chopped mixed fresh
  herbs, such as chives, parsley, basil
  and thyme

60ml/4 tbsp grated Parmesan cheese

60ml/4 tbsp olive oil

salt and ground black pepper

Wash the tomatoes. Slice off the tops, and scoop out the pulp. Chop the pulp and turn the tomatoes upside-down on a wire rack to drain. Place the pulp in a strainer, and allow the juices to drain off. Meanwhile, cook the pasta and drain 2 minutes before end of the recommended cooking time. Preheat the oven to 190°C/375°F/Gas 5. Combine the pasta with the remaining ingredients in a bowl. Stir in the drained tomato pulp. Season. Stuff the tomatoes, and replace the tops. Arrange them in one layer in a baking dish. Bake for 15–20 minutes. Serve hot or at room temperature.

MEDITERRANEAN SALAD WITH OLIVES AND CAPERS

A type of Salade Niçoise with pasta, conjuring up all the sunny flavours of the Mediterranean.

Serves 4

225g/8oz/2 cups chunky pasta shapes
175g/6oz/1 cup fine green beans
2 large ripe tomatoes
50g/2oz/2 cups fresh basil leaves
200g/7oz can tuna fish in oil, drained
2 hard-boiled eggs, shelled and sliced
*   or quartered*
50g/2oz can anchovy fillets, drained
30ml/2 tbsp capers
12 black olives, stoned

For the dressing

90ml/6 tbsp extra virgin olive oil
30ml/2 tbsp white wine vinegar or
*   lemon juice*
2 garlic cloves, crushed
2.5ml/½ tsp Dijon mustard
30ml/2 tbsp chopped fresh basil
salt and ground black pepper

Whisk all the ingredients for the dressing together and leave to infuse while you make the salad.

Cook the pasta in plenty of boiling salted water according to the manufacturer's instructions. Drain well and cool.

Trim the beans and blanch in boiling salted water for 3 minutes. Drain and refresh in cold water.

Slice or quarter the tomatoes and arrange on the bottom of a bowl. Toss with a little dressing and cover with a quarter of the basil leaves, then cover with the beans. Toss with a little more dressing and cover with a third of the remaining basil.

Cover with the pasta tossed in a little more dressing and half the remaining basil. Flake the tuna and arrange over the salad.

Arrange the eggs on top, then finally scatter over the anchovy fillets, capers and black olives. Pour over the remaining dressing and garnish with the remaining basil. Serve immediately. Don't be tempted to chill this salad – all the flavour will be dulled!

Fish Dishes

Together with tomatoes, herbs and capers, olives are
the perfect partner for fish. The flavour is excellent with
delicately flavoured trout and mullet as well as
more robust tuna or monkfish.

TUNA WITH TOMATOES AND OLIVES

A fresh, lemony marinade and an accompaniment of tomatoes and olives are perfect with rich, meaty tuna.

Serves 2

2 tuna steaks, about 175g/6oz each

90ml/6 tbsp olive oil

30ml/2 tbsp lemon juice

2 garlic cloves, chopped

5ml/1 tsp chopped fresh thyme

4 canned anchovy fillets, drained and
finely chopped

225g/8oz plum tomatoes, halved

30ml/2 tbsp chopped fresh parsley

10 black olives, stoned and chopped

ground black pepper

crusty bread, to serve

Place the tuna steaks in a shallow dish. Mix 60ml/4 tbsp of the oil with the lemon juice, garlic, thyme, anchovies and pepper. Pour over the tuna and leave to marinate for at least 1 hour.

Lift the tuna from the marinade and place on a grill rack. Grill for 4 minutes on each side, basting with the marinade, until the tuna feels firm. Meanwhile, heat the remaining oil in a frying pan. Add the tomatoes and fry for 2 minutes on each side. Divide the tomatoes between two serving plates and scatter the chopped parsley and olives over them. Top each with a tuna steak. Add the remaining marinade to the pan juices and warm through. Pour over the tomatoes and tuna steaks and serve at once with crusty bread.

COOK'S TIP

If you are unable to find fresh tuna steaks, you could replace them with salmon fillets, if you like – just cook them for one or two minutes more on each side.

MONKFISH WITH OLIVES AND TOMATOES

Monkfish, also known as angler fish, was once scorned by fishermen because of its huge ugly head,
yet now it is prized for its firm meaty texture – and is sometimes called "poor man's lobster".

Serves 4

750g/1¾lb monkfish tail, skinned
  and filleted
plain flour, for dusting
45–60ml/3–4 tbsp olive oil
125ml/4fl oz/½ cup dry white wine or
  fish stock
3 ripe tomatoes, peeled, seeded
  and chopped
2.5ml/½ tsp dried thyme
16 black olives (preferably Niçoise),
  stoned
15–30ml/1–2 tbsp capers, rinsed
  and drained
15ml/1 tbsp chopped fresh basil
salt and ground black pepper

Using a thin, sharp knife, remove any pinkish membrane and skin from the monkfish tail. Holding the knife at a 45° angle, cut the fillets diagonally into 12 slices.

Season the monkfish slices with salt and pepper and dust lightly with flour, shaking off any excess.

Heat a large heavy frying pan over a high heat until very hot. Add 45ml/3 tbsp of the oil and swirl to coat. Add the monkfish slices and reduce the heat to medium-high. Cook the monkfish for 1–2 minutes on each side, adding a little more oil if necessary, until lightly browned and the flesh is opaque. Transfer the fish to a warmed plate and keep warm while you make the sauce.

Add the wine or fish stock to the pan and boil for 1–2 minutes, stirring constantly. Add the tomatoes and thyme and cook for 2 minutes, then stir in the olives, capers and basil and cook for a further minute to heat through. Arrange three pieces of fish on each of four warmed plates. Spoon over the sauce and serve at once.

TROUT BAKED IN PAPER WITH OLIVES

Wrapping in paper packets means that fish will not dry out when baked, and all the flavour is retained.

Serves 4

*4 medium trout, about 275g/10oz
  each, cleaned*

75ml/5 tbsp olive oil

4 bay leaves

4 slices pancetta

60ml/4 tbsp chopped shallots

60ml/4 tbsp chopped fresh parsley

120ml/4fl oz/½ cup dry white wine

24 green olives, stoned

salt and ground black pepper

Preheat the oven to 200°C/400°F/Gas 6. Wash the trout well under cold running water. Drain. Pat dry with kitchen paper.

Lightly brush oil on to 4 pieces of baking parchment each large enough to enclose one fish. Lay one fish on each piece of oiled paper. Place a bay leaf inside each fish, and sprinkle with salt and pepper.

Wrap a slice of pancetta around each fish. Sprinkle with 15ml/1 tbsp each of chopped shallots and parsley. Drizzle each fish with 15ml/1 tbsp of oil and 30ml/2 tbsp of white wine. Add 6 olives to each packet.

Close the paper loosely around the fish, rolling the edges together to seal them completely. Bake the fish for 20–25 minutes. Place each packet on a plate and open at the table.

COOK'S TIP

If you can't find pancetta, use thinly sliced streaky bacon instead. Remove the rind before wrapping around the fish.

PAN-FRIED RED MULLET WITH OLIVE AND CAPER SAUCE

This spectacularly attractive and delicious dish is full of exciting and unusual flavours and is well worth the time it takes to prepare.

Serves 4

1 large fennel bulb

1 lemon

12 red mullet fillets, skin left intact

45ml/3 tbsp chopped fresh marjoram

45ml/3 tbsp olive oil

225g/8oz lamb's lettuce

salt and ground black pepper

For the vinaigrette

200ml/7fl oz/generous ¾ cup peanut oil

15ml/1 tbsp white wine vinegar

15ml/1 tbsp sherry vinegar

salt and ground black pepper

For the sauce

40g/1½ oz/⅜ cup black olives, stoned

15g/½oz/1 tbsp unsalted butter

25g/1oz/1 tbsp capers

Trim the fennel bulb and cut it into fine strips. Peel the lemon thinly, without any pith, then cut it into fine strips. Blanch the rind and refresh it immediately in cold water. Drain.

Make the vinaigrette by placing all the ingredients in a small bowl and lightly whisking until well mixed.

Sprinkle the red mullet fillets with salt, pepper and the chopped marjoram, and set aside.

Heat a wok and add the olive oil. When the oil is very hot, add the fennel and stir-fry for 1 minute, then drain and remove. Reheat the wok and, when the oil is hot, stir-fry the red mullet fillets, cooking them skin-side down first for 2 minutes, then cook the other side for 1 further minute. Drain well on kitchen paper and wipe the wok clean with kitchen paper.

For the sauce, cut the olives into slivers. Heat the wok and add the butter. When the butter is hot, stir-fry the capers and olives for 1 minute. Toss the lamb's lettuce in the dressing. Arrange the fillets on a bed of lettuce, topped with the fennel and lemon, and serve with the olive and caper sauce.

Poultry and Meat

Olives are a delicious addition to simple chicken or turkey dishes, they create interesting flavour combinations in more complex dishes and are also perfect with richer meats such as duck and beef.

Turkey Cutlets with Olives

This quick and tasty dish, full of Mediterranean flavours, makes a good light main course when served with a green vegetable or salad.

Serves 4

90ml/6 tbsp olive oil

1 garlic clove, peeled and lightly crushed

1 dried chilli, lightly crushed

500g/1¼lb boneless turkey breast, cut into 5mm/¼in slices

120ml/4fl oz/½ cup dry white wine

4 tomatoes, peeled, seeded and cut into thin strips

about 24 black olives, stoned

salt and ground black pepper

6–8 leaves fresh basil, torn into pieces

Cook's tip

If you prefer, use a fresh chilli instead of the dried chilli. Remove the seeds and chop very finely. Chicken breasts can be used instead of turkey.

Heat 60ml/4 tbsp of the olive oil in a large frying pan. Add the garlic and dried chilli, and cook over a low heat until the garlic is golden.

Raise the heat to moderate. Place the turkey slices in the pan, and brown them lightly on both sides. Season with salt and pepper. The turkey will be cooked after about 2 minutes. Remove the turkey to a heated dish.

Discard the garlic and chilli. Add the wine, tomato strips and olives. Cook over a moderate heat for 3–4 minutes, scraping up any meat residue from the base of the pan.

Return the turkey to the pan. Sprinkle with the basil. Heat for about 30 seconds, and serve.

CHICKEN WITH OLIVES

Chicken breasts or turkey, veal or pork escalopes may be flattened for quick and even cooking. You can buy them ready prepared, but they are easy to do at home.

Serves 4

*4 skinless boneless chicken breasts,
 about 150–175g/5–6oz each*

1.5ml/¼ tsp cayenne pepper

*75–105ml/5–7 tbsp extra virgin
 olive oil*

1 garlic clove, finely chopped

16–24 black olives, stoned

6 ripe plum tomatoes, sliced

small handful fresh basil leaves

salt

Carefully remove the fillets (the long finger-shaped muscle on the back of each chicken breast) and reserve for another use.

Place each chicken breast between two sheets of greaseproof paper or clear film and pound with the flat side of a meat hammer or roll out with a rolling pin to flatten to about 1cm/½in thick. Season the chicken with salt and the cayenne pepper.

Heat 45–60ml/3–4 tbsp of olive oil in a large heavy frying pan over a medium-high heat. Add the chicken and cook for 4–5 minutes until golden brown and just cooked, turning once. Transfer the chicken to warmed serving plates and keep warm while you cook the tomatoes and olives.

Wipe out the frying pan and return to the heat. Add another 30–45ml/2–3 tbsp of olive oil and fry the garlic for 1 minute until golden and fragrant. Stir in the olives, cook for a further 1 minute, then stir in the tomatoes. Shred the basil leaves and stir into the olive and tomato mixture, then spoon it over the chicken and serve at once.

COOK'S TIP

If the tomato skins are at all tough, remove them by scoring the base of each tomato with a knife, then plunging them into boiling water for 45 seconds. The skin should simply peel off.

DUCK STEW WITH OLIVES

This is a delicious way to prepare duck. The sweetness of the onions balances the saltiness of the olives.

Serves 6–8

2 ducks, about 1.5kg/3¼lb each, quartered, or 8 duck leg quarters

225g/8oz baby onions

30ml/2 tbsp plain flour

350ml/12fl oz/1½ cups dry red wine

475ml/16fl oz/2 cups duck or chicken stock

bouquet garni

90g/3½oz/1 cup stoned green or black olives, or a combination

salt, if needed, and ground black pepper

COOK'S TIP

If you take the breasts from whole ducks for duck breast recipes, freeze the legs until you have enough for this stew, and make stock from the carcasses.

Cook the duck pieces in a frying pan for 10–12 minutes until well-browned, turning to colour evenly. Pour off the fat.

Heat 15ml/1 tbsp of the duck fat in a large flameproof casserole and cook the onions, covered, until evenly browned. Sprinkle with flour and continue cooking, uncovered, for 2 minutes. Add the wine, duck pieces, stock and bouquet garni. Simmer, covered, for about 40 minutes, stirring occasionally. Add the olives and cook for a further 20 minutes. Transfer the duck, onions and olives to a plate. Strain the cooking liquid, skim off the fat and return the liquid to the pan. Boil to reduce by about one third, then return the duck and vegetables to the casserole. Heat through and season to taste.

BEEF AND OLIVE STEW WITH RED WINE

This rich, hearty dish is good served with mashed potatoes or polenta.

Serves 6

75ml/5 tbsp olive oil

1.2kg/2¹/₂lb boneless beef chuck steak,
  cut into 4cm/1¹/₂in cubes

1 medium onion, very finely sliced

2 carrots, chopped

45ml/3 tbsp finely chopped fresh
  parsley

1 garlic clove, chopped

1 bay leaf

a few fresh thyme sprigs, or pinch of
  dried thyme leaves

pinch of ground nutmeg

250ml/8fl oz/1 cup red wine

400g/14oz can plum tomatoes,
  chopped, with their juice

120ml/4fl oz/¹/₂ cup beef or
  chicken stock

about 15 black olives, stoned
  and halved

1 large red pepper, cut into strips

salt and ground black pepper

Preheat the oven to 180°C/350°F/Gas 4. Heat 45ml/3 tbsp of the oil in a large casserole. Brown the meat then remove to a side plate. Add the remaining oil, onion and carrots. Cook over a low heat until the onion softens. Add the parsley and garlic, and cook for a further 3–4 minutes. Return the meat to the pan with the bay leaf, thyme and nutmeg. Add the wine and cook, stirring, for 4–5 minutes. Add the tomatoes, stock and olives. Season. Cover the casserole, and place in the centre of the preheated oven. Bake for 1½ hours. Remove the casserole from the oven. Stir in the strips of pepper. Return the casserole to the oven and cook, uncovered, for a further 30 minutes, or until the beef is tender.

Pasta, Breads and Grains

Pasta makes a perfect partner for olives –

especially when combined with tomatoes and herbs.

Olives are excellent too with all manner of breads and

grains, adding a wonderful, intense flavour.

SPAGHETTI WITH OLIVES AND CAPERS

Olives and capers add piquancy to this spicy sauce which originated in Italy. It can be quickly assembled using a few storecupboard staples.

Serves 4

60ml/4 tbsp olive oil
2 garlic cloves, finely chopped
small piece of dried chilli, crumbled
50g/2oz can anchovy fillets, chopped
350g/12oz tomatoes, fresh or
*   canned, chopped*
115g/4oz/1 cup stoned black olives
30ml/2 tbsp capers, rinsed
15ml/1 tbsp tomato purée
400g/14oz spaghetti
salt
30ml/2 tbsp chopped fresh parsley,
*   to serve*

Bring a large pan of water to the boil. Heat the oil in a large frying pan. Add the garlic and the dried chilli, and cook for 2–3 minutes until the garlic is just golden.

Add the anchovies and mash them into the garlic with a fork. Then add the tomatoes, olives, capers and tomato purée. Stir the sauce well and cook over a moderate heat.

Add salt to the boiling water, and put in the spaghetti. Stir, and cook until the pasta is just *al dente*. Drain.

Toss the spaghetti with the sauce. Raise the heat and cook for 3–4 minutes, stirring constantly. Sprinkle with parsley and serve.

CROSTINI WITH BLACK OLIVES

Crostini are little rounds of bread cut from a French stick and topped with savoury ingredients such as cheese, olive paste, anchovy, tomato or chicken liver, then grilled or baked.

Makes 8

1 large French stick cut into 16 slices,
* and toasted*
16 canned anchovy fillets
24 black olives, stoned and halved
1 fresh basil sprig, to garnish
salt and ground black pepper

For the tomato topping
30ml/2 tbsp olive oil
2 garlic cloves, chopped
4 tomatoes, skinned and chopped
15ml/1 tbsp chopped fresh basil
15ml/1 tbsp tomato purée

For the onion topping
1 onion, sliced
30ml/2 tbsp olive oil
5ml/1 tsp chopped fresh thyme
15ml/1 tbsp black olive paste

For the tomato topping, heat the oil and fry the garlic and tomatoes for 4 minutes. Stir in the basil, tomato purée and seasoning. Spoon a little tomato mixture on to half of the slices of bread. For the onion topping, fry the onion in the oil until golden. Add the thyme. Spread the olive paste over remaining bread. Top all the bread with anchovies and olives. Garnish with a basil sprig.

SPAGHETTI WITH BLACK OLIVE AND MUSHROOM SAUCE

Olives add wonderful flavour to this rich, dark, pungent sauce which is topped with sweet cherry tomatoes.

Serves 4

15ml/1 tbsp olive oil

1 garlic clove, chopped

225g/8oz mushrooms, chopped

150g/5oz/1¼ cups black olives, stoned

30ml/2 tbsp chopped fresh parsley

1 fresh red chilli, seeded and chopped

450g/1lb spaghetti

225g/8oz cherry tomatoes

slivers of Parmesan cheese, to
*   serve (optional)*

COOK'S TIP

Add shiitake mushrooms if you like, their excellent flavour and texture is ideally suited to this robust sauce.

Heat the oil in a large pan. Add the garlic and cook for 1 minute. Add the mushrooms, cover, and cook over a medium heat for 5 minutes.

Place the mushrooms in a blender or food processor with the olives, parsley and red chilli. Blend until smooth.

Cook the pasta in boiling salted water until *al dente*. Drain well and return to the pan. Add the olive mixture and toss together until the pasta is well coated. Cover and keep warm.

Heat an ungreased frying pan and shake the cherry tomatoes around until they start to split (about 2–3 minutes). Serve the pasta topped with the tomatoes and garnished with slivers of Parmesan, if liked.

ITALIAN OLIVE BREAD

This traditional Italian bread is called focaccia. It is made with olive oil and flavoured with a
Mediterranean mixture of olives, sun-dried tomatoes and dried thyme.

Makes 1 loaf
350g/12oz/3 cups strong plain flour
2.5ml/½ tsp salt
5ml/1 tsp easy-blend dried yeast
5ml/1 tsp dried thyme
45ml/3 tbsp olive oil
8 black or green olives, stoned
  and chopped
3 sun-dried tomatoes in oil, drained
  and chopped
crushed rock salt

Place the flour, salt, yeast and thyme in a bowl. Add 200ml/7fl oz/⅞ cup warm water and 30ml/2 tbsp oil. Mix to a dough and knead for 10 minutes. Place the dough in an oiled polythene bag. Seal and leave in a warm place for 2 hours, until the dough has doubled. Knead on a floured surface. Sprinkle over the olives and tomatoes and knead in well. Shape the dough into a long flat oval and place on a greased baking sheet. Cover and leave to rise for 45 minutes. Preheat the oven to 190°C/375°F/Gas 5. Press your finger several times into the dough, drizzle over the remaining olive oil and sprinkle with salt. Bake for 35–40 minutes, until the loaf is golden.

COOK'S TIP
If you prefer, use a mixture of
black, green and stuffed olives.
Dried basil or oregano can be
used instead of the thyme.

ARTICHOKE AND OLIVE FOCACCIA

*Focaccia makes an excellent base for a variety of toppings. Grill or bake and serve as a snack or
accompaniment to soup and salads.*

Makes 3

60ml/4 tbsp olive paste or tapenade

3 mini focaccia

1 small red pepper, halved and seeded

*275g/10oz bottled or canned artichoke
hearts, drained*

75g/3oz pepperoni, sliced

5ml/1 tsp dried oregano

Preheat the oven to 220°C/425°F/Gas 7. Spread the olive paste or tapenade
over the focaccia. Grill the red pepper until blackened, put in a
polythene bag, seal and cool for 10 minutes. Skin and cut into strips.

Cut the artichoke hearts into quarters and arrange evenly over the focaccia
with the sliced pepperoni.

Arrange the red pepper strips over the focaccia. Sprinkle with the
oregano. Place in the oven for 5–10 minutes until heated through.

ONION AND OLIVE FOCACCIA

A dazzling yellow bread that is light in texture and distinctive in flavour is topped with a colourful array of black olives, red onions and rosemary sprigs.

Makes 1 loaf

pinch of saffron threads

150ml/¼ pint/⅔ cup boiling water

225g/8oz/2 cups plain flour

2.5ml/½ tsp salt

5ml/1 tsp easy-blend dried yeast

15ml/1 tbsp olive oil

For the topping

2 garlic cloves, sliced

1 red onion, cut into thin wedges

rosemary sprigs

12 black olives, stoned and

  coarsely chopped

15ml/1 tbsp olive oil

Place the saffron in a heatproof jug and pour on the boiling water. Leave to stand and infuse until lukewarm.

Place the flour, salt, yeast and olive oil in a food processor. Turn on and gradually add the saffron and its liquid. Process until the mixture leaves the sides and dough forms into a ball.

Turn on to a floured board and knead for 10–15 minutes. Place in a bowl, cover and leave to rise for 30–40 minutes until doubled in size.

Punch down the risen dough on a lightly floured surface and roll out into an oval shape, 1cm/½in thick. Place on a lightly greased baking sheet and leave to rise for 20–30 minutes.

Preheat the oven to 200°C/400°F/Gas 6. Use your fingers to press small indentations all over the surface of the foccacia.

Cover with the topping ingredients, brush lightly with olive oil, and bake for 25 minutes or until the loaf sounds hollow when tapped on the bottom. Leave to cool on a wire rack.

FOUR SEASONS PIZZA

The topping on this pizza is divided into four quarters, one for each "season". If you can't find ready made pizza bases, make your own with pizza mix.

Serves 4

450g/1lb peeled plum tomatoes, fresh or canned, weighed whole, without extra juice

75ml/5 tbsp olive oil

115g/4oz/1 cup mushrooms, thinly sliced

1 garlic clove, finely chopped

4 × 20cm/8in pizza bases

350g/12oz/1¾ cups mozzarella, cut into small dice

4 thin slices of ham, cut into 5cm/2in squares

32 black olives, stoned and halved

8 artichoke hearts preserved in oil, drained and halved

5ml/1 tsp oregano leaves, fresh or dried

salt and ground black pepper

Preheat the oven to 240°C/475°F/Gas 9 at least 20 minutes before baking the pizzas. Strain the tomatoes through the medium holes of a food mill placed over a bowl, scraping in all the pulp.

Heat 30ml/2 tbsp of the oil and lightly sauté the mushrooms. Stir in the garlic and set aside.

Spread the puréed tomato on the prepared pizza bases, leaving the rim uncovered. Sprinkle each evenly with the mozzarella. Spread mushrooms over one quarter of each pizza.

Arrange the ham on another quarter, and the olives and artichoke hearts on the two remaining quarters. Sprinkle with oregano, salt and ground black pepper, and the remaining olive oil. Immediately place the pizzas in the oven. Bake for about 15–20 minutes, or until the pizza crusts are golden brown and the topping is bubbling.

PEPPERONI PIZZA

The vibrant flavours of fresh, crisp peppers, spicy sausage and tangy olives make a mouth-watering combination in this classic pizza. If you prefer, use 275g/10oz pizza mix instead.

Serves 2–4

For the sauce
30ml/2 tbsp olive oil
1 onion, finely chopped
1 garlic clove, crushed
400g/14oz can chopped tomatoes
15ml/1 tbsp tomato purée

For the pizza base
275g/10oz/2½ cups plain flour
2.5ml/½ tsp salt
5ml/1 tsp easy-blend dried yeast
30ml/2 tbsp olive oil

For the topping
½ red pepper, sliced into rings
½ yellow pepper, sliced into rings
½ green pepper, sliced into rings
150g/5oz mozzarella cheese, sliced
75g/3oz pepperoni
8 black olives, stoned
3 sun-dried tomatoes, chopped
2.5ml/½ tsp dried oregano
olive oil, for drizzling

To make the sauce, heat the oil in a saucepan and add the onion and garlic. Fry gently for about 6–7 minutes, until softened. Add the tomatoes and stir in the tomato purée. Bring to the boil and boil rapidly for 5 minutes, until reduced slightly. Remove the pan from the heat and leave to cool.

For the pizza base, lightly grease a 30cm/12in round pizza tray. Sift the flour and salt into a bowl. Sprinkle over the easy-blend dried yeast and make a well in the centre. Pour in 175ml/6fl oz/¾ cup warm water and the olive oil. Mix to a soft dough.

Place the dough on a lightly floured surface and knead for about 5–10 minutes, until smooth. Roll out to a 25cm/10in round, making the edges slightly thicker than the centre. Lift the dough on to the pizza tray.

Spread the tomato sauce over the dough and then top with the peppers and mozzarella cheese. Slice the pepperoni thinly and add to the dough with the black olives and tomatoes. Sprinkle over the oregano and drizzle with olive oil. Cover loosely and leave in a warm place for 30 minutes, until slightly risen. Meanwhile, preheat the oven to 220°C/425°F/Gas 7.

Bake for 25–30 minutes and serve hot straight from the tray.

MINI PIZZAS

These delicious little pizzas with a topping of olives and sun-dried tomatoes make a quick supper dish.

Makes 4

150g/5oz packet pizza mix

8 sun-dried tomatoes in olive oil,
  drained

50g/2oz/½ cup black olives, stoned

225g/8oz ripe tomatoes, sliced

50g/2oz/¼ cup goat's cheese

30ml/2 tbsp fresh basil leaves

Preheat the oven to 200°C/400°F/Gas 6. Make up the pizza base following the manufacturer's instructions on the packet.

Divide the dough into four and roll each piece out to a 13cm/5in disc. Place on a lightly oiled baking sheet.

Place the sun-dried tomatoes and olives in a blender or food processor and blend until smooth. Spread the mixture evenly over the pizza bases.

Top with the tomato slices and crumble the goat's cheese over them. Bake for 10–15 minutes. Sprinkle with the fresh basil and serve.

COOK'S TIP

To reduce the oil content, use sun-dried tomatoes without oil. Soak in water for about 30 minutes, and blend with the olives with a little soaking water. For an even quicker pizza, you could use a good quality shop-bought passata and spread over the pizza bases, instead of the sun-dried tomatoes.

GRILLED CIABATTA WITH MOZZARELLA, ONION AND OLIVES

Ciabatta is available in most supermarkets. It's delicious topped with onions, cheese and olives.

Makes 4

1 ciabatta loaf

60ml/4 tbsp red pesto

2 small onions

oil, for brushing

225g/8oz mozzarella cheese

8 black olives, stoned

Cut the bread in half horizontally and toast lightly until just golden. Spread with the red pesto.

Peel the onions and cut horizontally into thick slices. Brush with oil and grill for 3 minutes until lightly browned.

Slice the cheese and arrange over the bread. Lay the onion slices on top and scatter some olives over. Cut in half diagonally. Place under a hot grill for 2–3 minutes until the cheese melts and the onion browns.

PASTA WITH OLIVE AND TOMATO SAUCE

Roasted Mediterranean vegetables, with olives and tomatoes, make a delicious pasta sauce.

Serves 4

1 aubergine

2 courgettes

1 large onion

2 red or yellow peppers, seeded

450g/1lb tomatoes, preferably
  plum-type

2–3 garlic cloves, coarsely chopped

60ml/4 tbsp olive oil

300ml/½ pint/1¼ cups smooth
  tomato sauce

50g/2oz/½ cup black olives, stoned
  and halved

350–450g/¾–1lb dried pasta shapes,
  such as rigatoni or penne

salt and ground black pepper

15g/½oz/¼ cup shredded fresh basil,
  to garnish

Preheat a 240°C/475°F/Gas 9 oven. Cut the vegetables into 2.5–4cm/1–1½in chunks. Discard the tomato seeds. Spread out the vegetables in a large roasting tin. Sprinkle with the garlic and oil and mix evenly. Season with salt and pepper. Roast the vegetables for 30 minutes or until they are soft and browned. Stir halfway through.

Transfer the vegetables to a saucepan. Add the tomato sauce and olives. Bring a large pan of water to the boil. Add the pasta and cook until it is just *al dente*. Meanwhile, heat the tomato and roasted vegetable sauce. Taste and adjust the seasoning. Drain the pasta and return it to the pan. Add the tomato and vegetable sauce and stir to mix. Serve hot, sprinkled with the basil.

PAN BAGNA

This literally means "bathed bread" and is basically a Salade Niçoise stuffed into a baguette or roll.
The olive oil dressing soaks into the bread when it is left for an hour or so with a weight on top of it.

Makes 4

1 large baguette

150ml/¼ pint/⅔ cup French dressing

1 small onion, thinly sliced

3 tomatoes, sliced

1 small green or red pepper, seeded
* and sliced*

50g/2oz can anchovy fillets, drained

90g/3½oz can tuna fish, drained

50g/2oz/½ cup black olives, stoned
* and halved*

Split the baguette horizontally along one side without cutting all the way through the crust.

Open the bread out so that it lies flat and sprinkle the French dressing evenly over the cut sides.

Arrange the onion, tomatoes, green or red pepper, anchovies, tuna and olives on one side of the bread. Close the two halves, pressing them firmly together.

Wrap in clear film, lay a board on top, put a weight on it and leave for about 1 hour: as well as allowing the dressing to soak into the bread, this makes it easier to eat.

Cut the loaf diagonally into four equal portions.

MUSHROOM AND OLIVE RISOTTO

This delicious risotto is bursting with flavour. Tomatoes, olives and garlic add an authentic Italian touch.

Serves 4

30ml/2 tbsp sunflower oil

1 large onion, chopped

75g/3oz smoked bacon, chopped

350g/12oz Arborio or risotto rice

1–2 garlic cloves, crushed

15g/^{1}/$_2$oz/^{1}/$_4$ cup dried sliced
  mushrooms, soaked in a little
  boiling water

175g/6oz mixed fresh mushrooms

1.2 litres/2 pints/5 cups hot stock

a few sprigs of oregano or thyme

15g/^{1}/$_2$oz/1 tbsp butter

a little dry white wine

45ml/3 tbsp chopped, peeled tomato

8–10 black olives, stoned and
  quartered

salt and ground black pepper

thyme sprigs, to garnish

Heat the oil in a large, heavy-based pan with a lid. Gently cook the onion and bacon until the onion is tender and the bacon fat has run out.

Stir in the rice and garlic and cook over a high heat for 2–3 minutes. Add the dried mushrooms and their liquid, the fresh mushrooms and half the stock, the oregano and seasoning. Bring gently to the boil, then reduce the heat. Cover tightly and leave to cook. Check the liquid in the risotto occasionally by very gently stirring. If quite dry, slowly add more liquid. (Don't stir too often, as this lets the steam and flavour out.) Add more liquid as required until the rice is cooked, but not mushy. Just before serving, stir in the butter, white wine, tomato and olives. Garnish with thyme sprigs.

POLENTA, BAKED TOMATOES AND OLIVES

A staple of northern Italy, polenta is a nourishing, filling food, served here with a delicious fresh tomato and olive topping.

Serves 4–6

2 litres/3¹/₂ pints/9 cups water
500g/1¹/₄lb quick-cook polenta
12 large ripe plum tomatoes, sliced
4 garlic cloves, thinly sliced
30ml/2 tbsp chopped fresh oregano
  or marjoram
115g/4oz/¹/₂ cup black olives, stoned
30ml/2 tbsp olive oil
salt and ground black pepper

Place the water in a large saucepan and bring to the boil. Gradually whisk in the polenta and simmer for 5 minutes.

Remove the pan from the heat and pour the thickened polenta into a 23 × 33cm/9 × 13in Swiss roll tin. Smooth out the surface with a palette knife until level, and leave to cool.

Preheat the oven to 180°C/350°F/Gas 4. With a 7.5cm/3in round biscuit cutter, stamp out twelve rounds of polenta. Arrange them so that they slightly overlap in an oiled ovenproof dish.

Layer the tomatoes, garlic, oregano or marjoram and olives on top of the polenta, seasoning the layers as you go. Sprinkle with the olive oil, and bake uncovered for 30–35 minutes. Serve immediately.

COOK'S TIP
For added flavour, add a little grated cheese to the polenta just after simmering. Grated Parmesan cheese, Gruyère or Gorgonzola are all suitable.

INDEX